FRED WILSON
a conversation with
K. ANTHONY APPIAH

March 11–April 16, 2006

PACEWILDENSTEIN
32 EAST 57TH STREET NEW YORK NY 10022

FRAGMENTS OF A CONVERSATION.

Fred Wilson and K. Anthony Appiah

K. Anthony Appiah: The first time I remember hearing of your work was when you did the installation at the Maryland Historical Society in Baltimore in 1992. I think people were excited in part because you invented a new thing to do in the art world. Museum people had been thinking about what they were doing, particularly with ethnographic collections, having symposia, writing scholarly articles; and you really asked what we could learn by going into what was stored away in the collections and finding ways to display it that would tell us something about ourselves. I wonder how much of the installation grew out of your own earlier experience as a museum-based educator.

Fred Wilson: Well, I think that's where it really came from. Obviously I studied art history and so some of what I was doing came from an awareness of being tied to a lineage within art history. But it came more from my experience living and breathing in New York City and being in the museum, whether I was working there or visiting as an artist and a person of color: my experience of all these different kinds of roles within the museum is where this work came from really. In all of my work I am answering questions for myself and investigating around things I'm feeling. I'm exploring the questions that no one can answer but me, or questions that I don't see anyone else answering at the time. And since I'm not a scholar in any particular area but rather someone working in an area that I sort of created for myself, my way of bringing it into the world is through my art work. I don't

expect to come up with answers. I just expect people to take away what they can, what they will; and then ask their own questions and make their own conclusions, take it in directions that I can't take.

KAA: So let's just talk a little about what you actually do in the sort of installation you did in that Baltimore museum. You go into the collection—especially among the objects stored away that aren't on display—and you find things that they probably hadn't been planning to foreground before you came.

FW: Yes, and I am sure the director didn't even know they had some of the things that I found.

KAA: Some of them had to do with the history of slavery and race in Maryland. Do you think they had any idea that that's what you'd find? What do you think they expected?

FW: I don't know. I was younger back then and never having done that kind of thing before or worked with museum people at that level before, I was not really deciphering what they were thinking. The project grew out of an invitation from Baltimore's museum for contemporary art, called The Contemporary. At that time they were a museum without walls. They would invite artists to create a work anywhere in Baltimore. The Contemporary knew I mimicked museum display in my installations. They knew I critiqued museums in my work, so they thought it would be great if I got to work in a real museum with a real museum collection. It was a collaboration between The

Contemporary, which sponsored the exhibition and created a contemporary art framework for it, and the Maryland Historical Society which had the collection and housed the exhibition. The only thing I do know is that the curator—Lisa Corrin—and the director of the museum—George Ciscle—told me afterward that, when they were trying to find a place for me to work—or even before that when they were just thinking about my coming to Baltimore to do a project—they had a conversation with the director of the Maryland Historical Society who said to them: "How do I make Chippendale furniture relevant to black children?" And the light bulbs went off in their heads.

KAA: So what do you think the Historical Society expected you to do?

FW: Well, I think they thought I would do a typical Black History Month show. I'm sure they thought I'd pull things from their collection and perhaps get things from other collections around Maryland. There are so many collections in the Washington and Maryland area that have lots of stuff relevant to African-American history. I mean the Douglass House is there in D.C., for example, so there's just lots of material that I could have used. But I suspect he was thinking not so much about the project as about trying to bring in "the community." You know Baltimore is at least 75% African American. So the director of the Historical Society was trying to do something to relate to the black community and he just felt really he didn't know how to do it and he knew it was something he had to do. There were very, very few black people going to the Maryland Historical Society at that time, so he was kind of clueless as to what do. And so this was a really great little moment for all these things to come together.

KAA: But what you put on display was not the sort of things that we're used to in Black History Month. Because it is normally, so to speak, about great men and women of color. So it's about celebration and positivity. But your installation showed people the real material remains of black life in Maryland, including the chains that had been used to bind the slaves. But it brought in black Baltimoreans anyway.

FW: Oh, it brought in everybody yes. I specifically didn't want to find things from outside the collection. I wanted to unpack it right there and their history in relationship to it, which would say a lot about Baltimore in general and the country in general and museums in general. And the show did bring in a lot of people. The museum people were nervous all along the way, which you could well imagine. I mean this was the first museum I worked with, so they didn't have a model for what I would do. But you see, all along I talked with people in Baltimore. I didn't just work at the museum. I needed to know how people were going to respond, because I am not from Baltimore and so I talked with the various community groups, with the museum people, everybody in the museum, everybody from the cleaning staff to the chairman of the board. I tried to understand all the positions, not so much to collaborate with *them*, but just to get a sense of where *I* was. So I wasn't working in a vacuum. I was trying to anticipate, perhaps unconsciously, how people would respond, be they black or white.

And I think that had a lot to do with the tenor of the exhibition that made it palatable for different kinds of visitors. I don't know if "palatable" is the right word, but I wanted to present difficult material in a way the visitors could take it in and not shut it out. One of the interesting things that happened, which I hadn't anticipated, was that as word got around Baltimore, people heard that even though this is about Baltimore and Maryland and American history, all the specificities of the collection were tied to individuals in Baltimore. I had no idea about this. I mean my assistant—she was an artist who was helping me—she just had to have her mother come to see the show. Well, her mother came to the opening. She brought her mother right over to the shackles and the silver (fig. 1). Her mother had donated the silver!

fig. 1:

Metalwork 1793–1880, from *Mining the Museum: An Installation by Fred Wilson*, 1992, The Contemporary and Maryland Historical Society, Baltimore.

There were these runaway slave broadsides that I reproduced (fig. 2). The family of the man who was trying to catch the slaves was still in Baltimore. In fact, one of the family members was the art editor of the local newspaper. So this was real to them. They recognized the street names, the family names, because it was all there in the artifacts on display. You know, I was there a year working on this project, off and on. I had no idea what it meant to the community. I knew this history, but I had no idea how it was so tied to that community. So I think people came out of the woodwork because of that as well.

The stories go on and on. There was a woman who worked in the museum in the education department. She was quite helpful. All of them were helpful actually, but she was the most helpful from the beginning. Her name was Kit Tubman, a white lady in the education department who worked with children. Eventually I asked her, so you have a very interesting name. She said, well, my husband's family had owned Harriet Tubman.

fig. 2:
Broadsides, 1992 (detail)
four framed prints
Installation dimensions variable

KAA: Wow! I think it is interesting that she said that, but also that she even knew it.

FW: Well, yes, it was her husband's name so perhaps she did not particularly feel the weight of it in the same way.

KAA: Still, someone had to tell her.

FW: Her husband had to tell her. But you know it's like anything, if someone is famous and time passes it enriches you to know your ancestors were part of history, once you get over the shock of it. And I never asked her any more about it, but she worked in the education department and really knew a lot about Harriet Tubman and, as I said, she was very helpful to me. I believe she felt a responsibility to tell the story, as she knew it. But I don't think I ever met her husband.

KAA: But part of what is going on here is something that you have often talked and told about, which is the way who we are comes with us when we go into museums. So the experience of the museum is differentiated depending on your identity.

FW: Yes. Different audiences respond very differently depending on which part of the picture they think of as connected with them.

KAA: And how do you create a show that anybody who comes in can make sense of without being alienated?

FW: What I do is very fluid. It's not the way a museum organizes exhibitions. For me, hopefully the projects are not a "them and us" situation. And I do it without really soft-pedaling anything. There is no finger pointing. When I went to the Maryland Historical Society of course they were initially … well you can imagine what they would be like in the historical society in Maryland and they were exactly like that! Some of them were not thrilled with my presence. But I understand people's initial reaction to me in a certain way just because, you know, I live in the world. I guess how I've grown up to negotiate the world has helped me in the museum environment. It's helped me negotiate these relationships and eventually, even if they don't know if they are going to like what I am going to do, they like me. Museum people are very nice people. They are always polite. That's one nice thing about that environment. So I'm trying to make sure everybody has an experience that they can grow from, rather just pointing fingers at people.

I think that stems from feeling profoundly like an outsider in museum culture, myself. Now that I am more established, I feel exactly the opposite. But I realize that one can "read" an exhibition. And when it's not speaking to you, you know it.

Often whoever has organized the show is totally oblivious to the fact that they have a very specific point of view. They're not conscious of it, but it's a very specific audience that they're speaking to. So, I'm the reverse: overly aware that there are many different people coming to see my work.

KAA: Now another thing that you make clear through your work is how much the museum itself as a place shapes how we respond to it. There's a story you told me about a show you put on when you were running your own gallery. It makes very nicely the point that what happens in the museum space is shaped by the character of the space and by the character of the people coming in, as well as by the objects that are being presented; and people normally forget about that when they are curating a show. They often forget that they have in fact constructed the installation in such a way that a particular audience will make the most sense of it. They also tend not to take account of the fact that the space itself is doing a lot of work.

FW: Right. And I mean, the average person is not trained to read these things. The curators you think would be. But they are thinking about the individual works. They have a certain scholarship that goes along with their aesthetic understanding of the works in relation to each other, but it doesn't go beyond that as far as how the space affects the visitor. And then there's the whole institution itself, before you even enter it. It gives you a very strong perception of what you are supposed to think. So I try to play with that as much as I can and break people out of that a bit. I mean, in my first exhibition, which was called "Rooms with a View," I displayed art in three different spaces (p. 8; figs. 3-5). I took very similar art works, and put them in a contemporary gallery space, a small ethnographic museum space, and a "historic house." And even though this was in a former South Bronx public school, people came to it. You know, immediately, they thought they understood what they were looking at basically by the environment, not by the objects themselves. And then they made the slow realization that they were looking at similar objects by the same artists from space to space. That to me was really very exciting. I am really interested in juxtaposition because that is the way that I can visually expose these kinds of ideas.

KAA: You put the same very similar objects in these different spaces and people responded differently. Do you think they were noticing that they were responding differently or was it you watching them notice things.

FW: No, no. They came and told me.

KAA: But this was your hope, right? Your hope was that people would recognize that the way they respond to contemporary art works isn't just a matter of the intrinsic character of the art works; it's also about where and how they are presented.

FW: Yes. And I think that came through very clearly. I mean one curator said to me when

fig. 3:
Installation view, from *Rooms with a View, The Struggle Between Culture, Content and the Context of Art*, 1987–1988, Longwood Art Gallery, Bronx Council on the Arts, New York.

fig. 4:
Installation view, from *Rooms with a View, The Struggle Between Culture, Content and the Context of Art*, 1987–1988, Longwood Art Gallery, Bronx Council on the Arts, New York.

fig. 5:
Installation view, from *Rooms with a View, The Struggle Between Culture, Content and the Context of Art*, 1987–1988, Longwood Art Gallery, Bronx Council on the Arts, New York.

she was in the ethnographic space, "Oh, you have a collection of primitive art." And she went to the next room, this contemporary gallery space, where there were works by the same artist, who was someone she had actually exhibited in her gallery. So it was very pronounced and this was just great for me. I mean it was really great for me and for the artists, because it was so successful. So the artists in it didn't mind that I had used them to make a point!

Of course it was the South Bronx in the '80's and they weren't really worried about what happened in this exhibition, but still! Then we got reviews which explained people's experiences. Even local people coming to it, I mean they couldn't put into words in the same way, but they were aware that these were different, very different, environments; and it became very familiar to them that basically art work can exist in different environments and be changed by it.

KAA: In the Baltimore show, you took artifacts connected with slavery, and obviously, in this country of ours, that is going to lead to reflections on race and racial identity. But you have explored those issues in other ways. I mean you have used some collections of so-called black memorabilia—cookie jars in the form of "mammies," that kind of thing (figs. 6-8). Here again, these are things that people are very anxious about. I mean some black people think they should not be neglected, but destroyed.

FW: Even the white people who collect them are often a little bit embarrassed by the fact that they have these objects. And then there are black people who collect them, too.

KAA: I was thinking about what you said earlier about trying to make your shows open to as wide a range of audiences as possible. So, you want to do this in a way that it doesn't make anyone feel: "Hey this show is an attack on me."

FW: Right.

KAA: But how do you do that? I mean, how did you take those objects and put them in a framework that would allow both the black person who thinks that this stuff is all terrible and the black person who is collecting black memorabilia into the same space and feel that they were learning something.

FW: Well, I mean I should say that it's never 100% successful at either end! There are always going to be people who don't think there is anything to gain from shows like this. But for the most part I think where I am most successful in that regard is when I just present the facts, in juxtaposition. If I have two images or objects side by side a third thought is revealed. It is my thought, but it allows the viewer to enter into my thinking a bit, but come up with conclusions for themselves, as well. When I have an image that's alone, that's without any kind of mediating device, especially with these so called black collectibles, it has upset some people. Some black Americans have a problem with that, but also, on the flip side, I have to deal with some white Americans who have a very different understanding. Some think these things are cute. They would say that it reminded them of when they were a child, they thought it was funny or cute or whatever. This is, of course, disturbing.

You know, the more personal the work, the more I don't worry about how people are going to respond to it. But when I'm dealing with these iconic things that exist in our culture that we really don't think much about, I do try to think about how viewers will feel about it. Not so much because it changes what I do, but because I try to be as honest as I can with how I feel about it. Otherwise you know I'm really not communicating, I'm really not. It's just like having a conversation with somebody who is sitting in the room with me, and I am trying to be as honest as I can with the understanding of who they are, and then let it fall where

fig. 6:
For You, 1995
ceramic, candy wrapped in plastic and cardboard, 6 ½ x 8 ½ x 7 ⅜"

fig. 7:
Puppet, 1995
painted porcelain, 7 x 2 ½ x 2"

fig. 8:
Hot Sax, 1995
painted ceramic, 7 ¾ x 3 ¼ x 2 ½"

it may. I just think it has so much to do with who I am and how I have been able to survive in the real world. It's hard for me to even tease it out.

KAA: So, who *are* you?

FW: Yeah, who am I?

KAA: Well, let's start with a story you told me about an experience you had with some Maori people in New Zealand.

FW: We were in a Morai, their spiritual meeting place, where they greet you by singing a song. And then they expect you to sing a song that relates to who you are and your background. It was a difficult thought because I, personally, have not been able to choose between all the various backgrounds that make up me. African American, Caribbean, Indigenous … All are important to me, and all come out more strongly in one environment or another. I think everybody does this, but I don't think most people think about it, whereas it's something I think about a lot. So, anyway, in that moment, I had to choose one. That was kind of a fascinating moment. Basically, because I was on the spot, I blurted out "Amazing Grace"—the amount of it that I remembered! It was passable but I got through with it. And I was probably more surprised than they were. In fact, they weren't surprised at all. They enjoyed it. That's because the folks that I met were highly spiritual people. Christianity is certainly not unusual in the Islands. But it was a surprise to me.

KAA: So, what did you learn about who you were from what you ended up singing? It's such an interesting song because it's been so taken up in particular by African Americans. And yet of course it was written by an Englishman who was a captain of a slave ship.

FW: Oh my God. I never knew that.

KAA: And this is a song that reflects his eventual recognition that this was something he shouldn't have done, that the slave trade was sinful. So it has all this strange history but for most of us I think today it's just an expression of African American spirituality.

FW: Right. I mean, yeah, you think of spirituality and this is what came. All I can say is that it had to well up from a very deep place because I was bereft of any other source and I was very unconscious of how it came up. As you know, my mother's family is from the Caribbean. She is not African American. It was not a particularly strong song for her, although she was the one who was from the church-going side of the family. My father's side of the family was not. So I am assuming that it was something deep from my childhood but also a later kind of an understanding of the position of black people in the United States. So, I mean in a way it does represent both sides of my family.

KAA: So you've got an African American side and, like many African Americans, that side includes indigenous people and European as ancestors as well. And presumably that could be true in the Caribbean, too?

FW: That is completely true.

KAA: But different parts of your ancestry are foregrounded within those communities.

FW: Different parts. Sure. It is a joy when it happens.

KAA: Though, presumably it just has to be the fact that most of your life the first identity has got to be as an African American. And so part of what you are telling these New Zealanders was whatever else I am, I am African American.

FW: Still that song is very rooted in American history, which was a surprise, I have to say. I'm glad I came up with something so that we can have something to talk about! Because really I don't know where it came from, but I'm glad it was that. Even the religious connotations surprised me, because I've sort of put that behind me.

KAA: You grew up basically in New York.

FW: New York City, yes, and the suburbs of New York.

KAA: But while you were still under your mother's roof, you went to church.

FW: Yes.

KAA: Because that was the family thing. But were you conscious all along, because your mother was from the Caribbean, of a kind of distance from the normal African American experience?

FW: Oh yeah, my experience is pretty distant from that. My parents divorced when I was young so my father lived in Manhattan, but I was very close to my grandmother and my cousin on my father's side, who lived in the Bronx, and so when we moved to the Bronx from Westchester I saw them a lot. Later, when we were back in Westchester, I saw them less. I mean they were the people that I knew on that side of the family. I also had close contacts with the West Indian side of the family growing up. So, for most of my life, really the formative years which I have stated at other times, I was the only black child in the school or the neighborhood. And I think that heightens my view of myself as being an African American. It wasn't coming from my mother, who really didn't view the world in that way and really couldn't understand the world in that way because it was not her world. Although she married my father, she was kind of an outsider herself. So my connections with the African American side were from grandmother, my father's mother, who was very strongly rooted in New York. She came to Harlem in the 20's from the Midwest to go to NYU and so she was very much involved with and interested in education and Harlem Renaissance notions, not a religious person at all. My father was not a religious person at all, either. In fact, if I told him the story about those Maoris, he would be horrified (Fred chuckles).

KAA: I won't tell him!

FW: So that cultural history is more what my grandmother was deeply involved with and she felt very close with the "Negro" community. I once asked her about Marcus Garvey and I could tell that it was not a question that was going to go anywhere and that was not her. He was a little too radical, I suppose, for her. She lived in Sugar Hill you know, and she was very involved with Civil Rights in her way.

KAA: I have one more question that sort of arises from something in the New Zealand story. You are an American, obviously, and when you are outside the United States, that's the first thing that people think of you as.

FW: Right. Well, sometimes. I mean if I come representing the United States, then I come as an American. But if I'm just there, they wait to see. These days, if I don't open my mouth, people think of me as coming from North Africa when I'm in Europe.

KAA: That's not so great!

FW: I've been called Bin Ladin in Sweden! So, you know that also plays into how I make my work; I start with the understanding that context really changes everything.

KAA: Well, I was moving in the direction of talking about the work for the Biennale in Venice. There you inevitably think of yourself as representing your country. Was that the first time?

FW: No, the second time. I represented the United States in Egypt before that. And that was a whole other …

KAA: Talk about either of them.

FW: Well, I had already been to Egypt because I had lived with my father there for a brief period. And, when I was young, no one knew I wasn't Egyptian if I walked around, just because why would a young American be wandering around? They thought I was Egyptian, from the south. They just knew that I was from there. And people would ask me you know, "Where are you from?" I would say from the United States. "But where are you really from?" And I'd say, "Well I am really from the United States." They'd say, "Ask your father." Oh, this boy really doesn't know. "Just ask your father, he'll know where you are from out here." It becomes a long conversation which is always wonderful, wonderful to me because—as a side note—it was the first place I'd been where I didn't stand out.

KAA: I know what you mean. When I was a child, I was living between Ghana where I was lighter than everybody else, and England where I was darker than everybody else. So people looked at you both places. It's very interesting. But what you just said suggests, of course, that Egyptians think the U.S. is a white country.

FW: Oh, I mean at least they did. I mean now, I don't know. I'm wondering whether television and movies haven't exported a little more diversity, but I remember when I was in Aswan, up the Nile, this young veiled woman came over to me for some reason. I said I was American, and she said, "Oh yes, Dallas." She meant the TV show *Dallas*!

KAA: So tell me about the Cairo experience.

FW: Well, in Cairo, I did a project that was mostly about the West's view of Egypt, the European View and the American View and the African American view of Egypt historically. I was thinking, completely historically, not in contemporary terms, but I think it was read as a metaphor for the contemporary, which I wasn't expecting. And the State Department didn't mind my doing it because they were able to think of it as historical. But it was controversial. Well, I think this is largely why the United States gets involved in these things. We want people to know that America has an open discourse and we allow diverse points of view even if the State doesn't agree with it. But I was looking at Napoleon and Lord Nelson and basically the African American viewpoint. This was a moment when there was a lot of Egypto-African American regalia ... hats, and jewelry and lots of stuff, hip hop stuff. Michael Jackson had this video of himself as Tut and Magic Johnson as a pharaoh, and I had that playing there in the installation. I completely redesigned the gallery. The gallery used to be the Pasha's palace. To make it a modern space it had been renovated by putting white walls in front of the ornately ornamented gold, mirrored and wall-papered room. I simply reverted it to the palace. I repainted the walls. I got stuff from the Souk and refurnished it. I mean, I commissioned a local painter to copy pre-Raphaelite paintings, the whole thing. I got all these early books that I found around Cairo, Orientalist books and all the book marks that I put in them had these questions about Orientalism. All the artifacts had questions attached to them in Arabic about the Western view of Egypt, historically, but the questions would not be unlike today's questions so it really sort of leapt over time.

KAA: But this is interesting, because in the Biennale tradition people come from other places to represent those places and so the standard exhibition ignores the place that it's in.

FW: Right.

KAA: So, you bring a current, let's say, French artist.

FW: That's right.

KAA: And you dump his work down in the Prado, or somewhere.

FW: Right.

KAA: But in Cairo, you took account of the place.

FW: That's right. But this is what I do in the States, too. So wherever I go, what they get to see is this kind of practice ... if they could step back from it, anyway. The difficulty in Cairo was that at first they thought, "Who's this American talking about us?" I'm talking about the intelligentsia. But I went there three or four times, so they got to know me a little bit and the fact that I am African American was ultimately really a good thing in this situation, considering what I was doing. It was extremely popular with some and others were rather nervous about it, I guess because of my naivety about what was under the surface in contemporary Egypt and the Middle East. Here I was talking about something that related to that present, but not directly talking about it. So all the huge number of people that go to the Biennale, all the university students, just loved seeing things that they had never seen. The young folks didn't know anything about Orientalism; they didn't know anything about Michael Jackson, especially the scantily clad dancers in music videos. All of these things had nothing to do with their contemporary world. In many ways the Egyptian art community didn't know what to do with me because they hadn't seen this form of installation.

Things have changed now because of these international exhibitions. In the art schools there, most of the works used to look like bad

Picassos or whatever. But now I think things have changed. So my saying this room *was* the artwork; and these voices emanating from pots *were* the art; these Orientalist books *were* part of the artwork. You know, this was all new and kind of made some of the older faculty nervous. They can't talk about that with the students. It messed with their whole sense of what art is. But there were other artists, young artists who saw this as a route for things they could do outside the academy; because there is basically no art market, all they have is the academy.

Whenever I do a project outside the United States, I have to realize that they see me as an American and then they see whatever they think of me when they look at me, and if they see me as African American or Black American, then another thing gets laid on me, and that's just the way it goes. But when you're representing the United States, it's much more intense.

FW: In Venice, the United States knew exactly what I was going to propose. I actually did exactly what I said I was going to do. I could have changed it along the way, but this was what I was interested in doing, looking at the African presence in Venice in the early centuries until now. The Venetians and the Italians were fascinated, and were not afraid of this foreigner doing it. The one time something like that came up was with an art dealer when I wanted to borrow some paintings. In the exhibition I had three historical paintings, one Tiepolo and a couple of other lesser-known works, which had a servant character in them. And the dealer, really a wonderful man, loaned the paintings, which amazes me, because you know they were very valuable paintings. I told him what the project was going to be and the paintings I wanted and that I was going to have these voices emanating from the African

fig. 9:
Shatter
from *Fred Wilson: Speak of Me as I Am*, 2003, United States Pavilion, 50th Venice Biennale, organized by the List Visual Arts Center, Massachusetts Institute of Technology, Cambridge.

fig. 10:
Spark
from *Fred Wilson: Speak of Me as I Am*, 2003, United States Pavilion, 50th Venice Biennale, organized by the List Visual Arts Center, Massachusetts Institute of Technology, Cambridge.

fig. 11:
Faith's Fate
from *Fred Wilson: Speak of Me as I Am*, 2003, United States Pavilion, 50th Venice Biennale, organized by the List Visual Arts Center, Massachusetts Institute of Technology, Cambridge.

figure in the painting, and he said, "Whose voices? Is it an Italian voice, an American voice, you know, whose voice is this going to be from the paintings?" Well, I just said, "I'm imagining an African voice from that period, so hopefully it's neither or both." And so he was the one person who directly questioned from whose position this is coming and how are you going to represent this. Some Americans also wondered how this was going to happen and I just basically wanted to just see if I could imagine a voice for these people who have no voice. They're in the paintings, but who are they? There's nothing written about them.

I feel the African presence for the Venetians was closer. There's imagery of Africans on the door knockers; in the hotels, there are fancy carved servant characters and it's really all throughout the society (figs. 9-11). Their representation was closer to the American representation of Native Americans, more like Pocahontas, or corporate use of tribal names like Cherokee Jeeps, kind of exotic …as in—we don't know any of these people, but it represents us because no place else has this culture in its history. It's not the same kind of mammy and pappy imagery; it's more exotic imagery that's considered kind of safe …

KAA: And they're less anxious with their own relationship to it?

FW: Yeah, totally, they have no self-consciousness about it, it's just there. Someone wrote in the guest book—I think it was an English critic who was really offended by the exhibition— "You know, you don't know anything about European history."

KAA: This is someone who interrupted you as saying, "Naughty Venetians, they had black folk as servants."

FW: Yeah, yeah, yeah. And of course they interpreted me as saying the black figures were like slaves in the Americas, which of course they were not. Anyway this is a history that has never been written, how could he know it. I mean I'm not writing a history book. I think it was well received by the Americans and Europeans who saw it, but some Americans were looking for something exactly like the American history only in Italy. So they expected me to do something that was visceral when it's not the same history, and I was not going to represent it that way. One European art critic looked at me incredulously and said "this is like a European artist did this." I took this as a compliment. I think it did not look like American art to him, whatever that is. This kind of site-specific project that I do really works with the site. I immerse myself in the place and the culture. People coming into it from distant places don't always understand the specificity of it.

KAA: But nevertheless, the Venetians were happy because, here was someone who came from America and said, "I've noticed that I'm in Venice and that I'm going to respond to my environment."

FW: Right. And of course, in every project, I do my homework. I talk to many people and I learn a great deal about the history from the average person as well as the scholar. But, you know, it's art; and in Europe a lot of latitude is given to art. Here in the United States, people like things pinned down, they like to have it all explained; whereas Europe is not quite like that. And so the Venetians really enjoyed this piece being about Venice but also this history they didn't know …

KAA: Now in Venice—a city with a great history of artistry in glass—there was some work in your show that was based on things you had already started doing with glassblowers in Seattle.

FW: And I should say that one piece, this chandelier, is going to be in the Pace show, too. But I think I wasn't afraid to go to Murano—where Venetians have been making glass for seven hundred years—because I already had an understanding of glass. So there really was a wonderful dovetailing of timing for me. Because I had worked in Seattle with glassblowers and realized there this was a medium I could speak through, I had some ideas about it already and so when I got to Venice, it was a no-brainer to go to Murano. So rather than just buy things, I actually had things produced. And, as I said, Europeans are used to artists and they're very kind of fluid in Italy, so they were fine with whatever I wanted them to make. And what I asked them to make was something they could easily make, so it was quite fine. When I told the man what I wanted to make, he showed me the chandeliers he had, and I said, "I want that one, I want it really huge." It was a sort of 18th century-style chandelier. He said, "Oh yes, I could do that, no problem." I told him I wanted it in black glass, and he said, "You want what? Oh, there's no problem. No, no!"

KAA: He would understand that you're an artist.

FW: Yeah, yeah, yeah.

KAA: So of course you'll want it in black.

FW: Yes, and they thought it was fine. In fact, the response now is that they have made their own version with gold all around it. Still black but with gold on it. For me that particular piece was really emblematic of the whole exhibition, really brought all those ideas together and not only because it's using the color black on a Venetian form, but it's also kind of sad and funereal and kind of spooky … it connects with the Othello story. Verbally, visually, the whole thing. In the show, there were four videos of Othello, four movies going backwards and this audio collage of two operas and two plays of the death scene.

KAA: Can we think about the Venice project a little bit in terms of your trajectory? More and more you're making objects rather than simply working with objects that were already there, which is how you started out in Baltimore. So we start with you just rummaging around in the basement in Baltimore, taking somebody's collection and telling us something about the place and the country by displaying it in a certain way. Then you move to taking objects that are out there and making a collection of your own. Again, telling us something about identity and race and the country. But now you're making all kinds of things. Or rather having objects made. I'm interested in the Pace show in part because it's one thing to make an object for an installation, because that connects with what you've been doing already, but these objects are now free from their original context. Now we're just going to have the chandelier. It was made to talk about blackness in Venice, and, of course, it's an exciting way to represent blackness in Venice, to take something from Murano and do something that's always been done in white in black.

FW: Right.

KAA: And now, in this show, the Pace show, you're going to have more glass, which has never been part of one of your museum installations. So the new works are not about collection any more at all. And while they'll be installed together, they each have their own independent life and they weren't made in order to be installed in relation to one another.

FW: That's right.

KAA: So you're moving now toward creating in a way, more free-standing objects. But there's still the issue of the relationship between the identity of the viewer and the identity of the object and the identity of the space that it's in. Talk about that a little bit.

FW: Well, you said something there that … well, I had thought about it a long time ago, but I hadn't really thought about it lately, just in the middle of working on this project. Working with a collection, there is a theme and it becomes finite because of the outside limitations—what's in the collection; and then when I collected those collectibles, I was collecting these things myself, but I still worked thematically in a certain way. I think that the way I work, you know, is that I move from one set of ideas and go through them, all the way through them.

I think I am also becoming much more comfortable in the commercial gallery environment. What I mean by comfortable is that it's not pretending to be some other kind of space, it is what it is, and I'm within that space and to some degree speaking to it. Certainly having a show called "Collectibles," in a gallery that sells things (the Metro Pictures gallery in 1995) was on one level about collecting and about people who buy. What they buy and why they buy it and all those kind of things. But this is even a step further in that it has nothing to do with anything out in the real world except what's going on in my head … which can be a frightening thing for me when it comes out. So, with this particular project—which has been a long time coming and I've spent a long time thinking about it—I was more and more thinking about just the notion of blackness and what is black and what really does that mean? And should that be something in the 21st century? Should blackness have as much meaning as it does and how negative and how positive is it? And what are the other connections to this term and to this color and is it something that is so reductive that it's a problem or is it so reductive that it sort of makes blood rush in a certain way so that it's positive or can it be all these things at once? And so I'm just trying to tease it out in this way.

I mean think about the glass drips. In Venice, they went along with the chandelier because of a kind of sadness (fig. 12) … I mean I view them as tears on one level, black tears. There's a line in Othello,

drop tears as fast as the Arabian trees Their med'cinable gum.

So that was kind of a nice intersection for me, but actually I became interested in trying to just use this, use the blackness as a positive and a negative or just put it all out there. Take it apart so maybe that will dissipate the meaning rather than solidifying it. Because in the United States it has been so culturally encoded. Much like "Amazing Grace," its starting point was not a good one, but it has become internalized as a positive and so I like to look at that. And so the chandelier is in the exhibition because Shakespeare's Othello, though set in Venice, is known by most people in America. It embodies a dilemma and an image for contemporary people of African descent that relates directly to my interest in the notions of "black." Shakespeare used the image of blackness in opposition to Desdemona's whiteness, which clearly can be understood today. Othello's chandelier also suggests the effect of power and empire on the fate of African people. For me, its monstrous melancholy goes hand in hand with its beauty. It used to be the trials and tribulations, as well as the successes of any group of people was only known to a few, now everything is globalized, we are all connected. The beauty and the horror are magnified because we can see and feel that we are all a part of it, as it happens. This sculpture, the chandelier, though designed from one first made during the Venetian Empire, can be seen as a metaphor for contemporary conundrums of power and blackness. It fits right in with my continued interests. And not everybody got to Venice, and I really want people to see this object.

I do think with this exhibition the discussion of blackness will revolve around race issues that control identity by reducing it to this color, and the stereotypes associated with the color in relation to other materials which I grew up with in the United States: tar, oil, ink. All that negative imagery was in my upbringing—which now I realize, because I have had a lot of students, that this has totally nothing to do with them—but it's still a part of mine, unfortunately. But then talking about oil has a new currency. One can find these kinds of strange paths, which I'm interested in marking. There's a piece that I plan to do soon which is a globe, the "starlight" globe as they're called. I'm using these black globes that light up and adding chandelier parts. The chandelier parts will demarcate slave routes and oil routes, consuming countries and producing countries. And not only American slavery, but I'm looking at the Mediterranean and the Middle East, and then seeing how they overlap. I mean they probably don't have any direct relationship, but I'm interested in how "natural resources" have been exploited by great powers and their effect on global economies, not to mention conflict. This led me to looking at the diamond industry and other gems. I'm creating a royal crown (and then maybe a tiara, of another European queen) with real black gems. In addition to the exploitation of people and the landscape through mining, I've been thinking about the Middle East, and Great Britain's involvement in early oil production. I haven't made this thing yet, but I was thinking of hiding a design of gems on the crown: BP, you know, black people, you know British Petroleum.

I think it makes the most sense to use actual gems, for many reasons. I've never really considered using fake gems made of glass, even though it would be in sync with the rest of my work.

KAA: But one thing that's striking to me, having seen the Drips—the black drops of glass—is something that I think is kind of new in your work which is a kind of concern with what I might call the character of the material that you're working with.

FW: Yes.

KAA: Because now you're actually working with this stuff.

FW: Yes, with glassblowers in Seattle.

KAA: And it's weird stuff. I mean from a technical, physical point of view, it's actually a liquid.

FW: That's right.

KAA: But behaves like a solid in some ways. And—this is something that Murano has played on, for centuries and centuries—it's something that seems to naturally attract the human eye and it's also reflective, so that it gives you back images, and all of these properties of it suggest that it's actually quite a difficult substance to use to communicate, because it's already got all these layers of natural significance and I wonder if that doesn't put you off. Or does it make it attractive?

FW: Well it's a challenge. I like the challenge. I am very interested in beauty, even with my museum projects, you know, the installations; I think they're very physically beautiful, aesthetically pleasing. But I use beauty in service to meaning and beauty as a seductive material that draws you in, so that you're there and you can deal with the subject matter or at least you're drawn in, and then you *have* to deal with the subject matter. So that's another thing that I like, you just can't let yourself get swallowed up by beauty. It's a tightrope walk that I try to do and so that is the tricky part with using glass because it's very seductive and no matter what you do it's a beautiful thing. But it could be really facile also. So as an artist, for me, it's not that interesting, if I know exactly what's going to happen. If I feel extremely, completely comfortable, it makes me nervous. If I'm completely comfortable with it, then maybe I won't push myself. I am very unsure about how people see this work, and I constantly re-evaluate how I see it and I think that's really important for an artist; it

fig. 12:
Chandelier Mori
from *Fred Wilson: Speak of Me as I Am*, 2003, United States Pavilion, 50th Venice Biennale, organized by the List Visual Arts Center, Massachusetts Institute of Technology, Cambridge.

keeps you making work, keeps you pushing it, it keeps you thinking about it, and so yeah, if there are limitations, if there's something complicated, I sort of go toward that.

KAA: One thing that you've done with the Drips, to interrupt what you might call the easy pleasure, is to put those little eyes on the drops (opposite page). They could be just beautiful objects to contemplate and empty your mind into it … but those little details, they stop that.

FW: I could not leave it just like that for people to completely miss my underlying feeling about it. I have to put in these spots, those eyes. They're kind of silly, but they also have this other history to them and that's why they don't all have eyes. It's not just enough that you realize this is not just about the colors, not just about the material; it's not just about sperm and eggs, or not just about a beautiful object; there's this other culturally inscribed thing that I'm forcing you to see, because I have to see it.

KAA: You mean the connection with the "mammy's" eyes in the collectibles?

FW: Yes. And I don't think I would have done this had I not collected the memorabilia for the project that I did. I collected them because I didn't like them and I wanted to understand why I didn't like them. That's why I made all these projects with them; at a certain level, you collect things and it kind of numbs you to what's problematic about them. I don't think collecting them is the way to go for me personally. But I think it allowed me to make these works. In this project, I'm sort of pulling all this stuff out in the hope of reaching an end to it …I do envision there will be a last piece that will reveal itself as the last piece and I have some ideas about that … we'll get into a glass works studio and we'll see if it happens!

KAA: But this is partly about getting the black memorabilia out of your system?

FW: Yes. And all the memories of racism in its various forms that I have. And you know, obviously, I won't actually get it out of my system. But it *is* about that, and that was what the collectibles works were about too, and I guess that's what all these projects are about—well this is slightly different from the museums and stuff—but still it's about unpacking this stuff around me that is kind of telling me who I am and telling me about the world. So I can ask if this is true and do I really believe in this. How much have I internalized? I find that out by looking at it from various angles and that's what this is.

KAA: Among the other things you made for Venice which was also in your last show at the Aldrich, "Black Like Me," there are these black and white walls (p. 21) … is that glass, too?

FW: Ceramic tile. But the glazing is glass.

KAA: But that's moving onward in terms of materials, it's different from glass.

FW: It is, yes, and it kind of sits apart, but because it's black and white and shiny, it sort of has a relationship to it. I see myself moving in ceramics, this way. I did the first tile wall for a show in Manhattan. That was the first wall like that; and then I was thinking about tile in Venice. There's tile everywhere in Venice and of course tile all over the Muslim world. If I do this at Pace, and I'm using various institutional kinds of tile, I am thinking about institutional spaces or spaces that are not private spaces, although in the piece in Venice and at the Aldrich—in the "Black Like Me" show—all the writing in the grout is very much like what you'd find in a men's room: speaking out to the world, though nobody knows you're doing it, who

Pssst!, 2005
blown glass
3" height x 12" diameter

you are (fig. 13). It's very anonymous, that's the kind of environment that I'm thinking about and the next piece would really be like a cage, more like tile, wall, floor and either bars or more likely fencing. This is where I'm thinking these days, where it's going: Guantánamo Bay perhaps.

But there's another completely different strand of thought that plays into this. In Hanover, New Hampshire—where I was doing an installation at Dartmouth's Hood Museum—I came across all these busts from the early part of the 20th century, from the World's Fair in 1904 in St. Louis (p. 22; fig. 14). They were made by the American Museum of Natural History and sold to various museums, but I was shocked to find out they were cast directly on people's faces at the World's Fair. Faces of various races, and they're not happy. You can see in their faces that they are not happy with their situation. So I went back to the museum and learned a little more: one of these busts looked very familiar to me, and it indeed was Ota Benga.

fig. 13:
Turbulance, 2001 (detail)

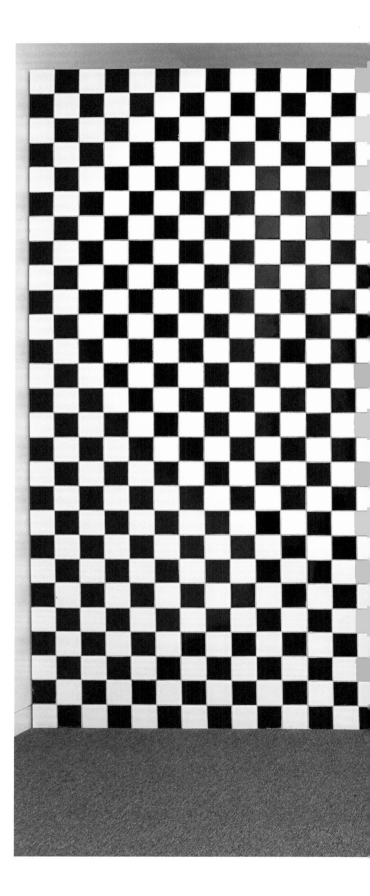

Turbulence, 2001
tile wall, graphite, ink, two audio recordings, electronics, and light
9' 10" x 18' x 4 ½"

Vanity, 2005
wood, plate glass, glass hardware
60 x 45 x 22 ½"

KAA: Oh wow!

FW: Ota Benga, the Pygmy who was brought from the Belgian Congo and exhibited at the World's Fair in St. Louis (fig. 15). I've been thinking about the fact that he was in a cage; about the plight of Pygmies, even today. So all these ideas I think are swirling around and may come into this kind of space. I like the fact that I can use the tile and re-use it and use certain elements like the sound—I used the tapes of *Othello*, the play and the opera, from Venice with the tiled wall at the Aldrich—and the writing on the grout, but re-fashion it and it has a slightly different meaning.

KAA: But what brought you to this idea in the first place?

FW: You know that's a good question. Oh, I remember, but it had nothing to do with content, it was the visual. I was in San Francisco and I saw a tile wall that was black and white tile and it had an incredible optical illusion and I really wondered what was happening with that. I thought that was really interesting to me: it's black and white tile and of course, you know, extrapolating black and white and

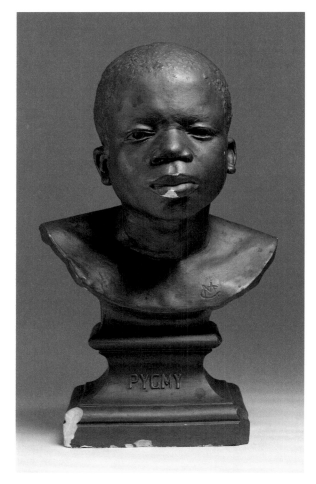

fig. 15:
Caspar Mayer (American, 1871–1931)
Bust of Ota Benga, a Bachichi man
early 20th century
plaster
Hood Museum of Art, Dartmouth College, Hanover, New Hampshire; gift of the American Museum of Natural History.

this kind of optical difficulty, that's where it kind of began. I tuck away ideas a lot and I write down ideas and they don't come out till later, till the raw idea becomes meaningful.

KAA: You mentioned to me earlier that you had been in Ghana, where I grew up.

FW: That's right, 30 years ago.

KAA: As a very young man, we should say!

FW: That's right. In the stroller!

KAA: And you went to the north of Ghana and saw those amazing, almost spherical, pots that they make.

fig. 14:
Installation view, **Lifecast Busts from the Louisiana Purchase Exposition, St. Louis, 1904,** from *Fred Wilson: So Much Trouble in the World—Believe It or Not!,* 2005, Hood Museum of Art, Dartmouth College, Hanover, New Hampshire. Hood Museum of Art, Dartmouth College, Hanover, New Hampshire; gift of the American Museum of Natural History.

FW: Well, first you see the structures they live in, which are terracotta pots, essentially. And then the pots that the women make. What I found really fascinating was that after they make them, they sit them on their lap, and it looks like an extension of their bodies. It looks like a pregnant woman. I have made some big pots already, which I don't think I'm going to have in the Pace show, but you never know. I wanted to make a pot that you could live in. And the pots that I made, really right after September 11th, I call them safe houses, are a kind of comfortable environment (fig. 16). I was thinking a lot about my mother also, who's not well at all, and she's not going to get better. So I was just thinking about the pregnant body, and as space to sort of hide in, and this form that I'm really attracted to. It took me a while to figure out why I was so attracted to the form and if it was specifically from my experience in Ghana. So I went looking at many different kinds of ceramic domestic pottery from around the world to see what form really I had this feeling for. It is those Ghanaian pots, as it turns out. So I'm going to continue doing that.

KAA: But there it's more the shape than the material.

FW: It's very much the shape. But I think it also is the material. In Venice I had a big pot, but it was black. It was a Tuscan pot, which I blackened for the project. I didn't glaze the pot the black color, I stained it. It had a matte finish. I like the fact that the clay material is kind of the opposite of glass which is shiny and has this sensational beauty to it. I'm interested in domestic pottery which is the opposite of that.

KAA: But was the one that you blackened in Venice the first one that you put in a show?

FW: No, I made one up in Alfred, New York. I sort of created this residency for myself. I told them I'd come there and teach if they let me borrow their students. And I went up there and gave a couple of lectures and just stayed up there. I created work for an exhibition in their gallery. The students, particularly a grad student named Gregg Moore, made this huge pot for me—a ceramic pot—and it was not too long after September 11th, so the whole exhibition was a lot about that … I mean the whole notion of finding a safe place in an unstable world was on my mind. It was still in my mind two years later when I was in Venice. Certainly Africans in Italy of the 12th and 13th century had no more stability than they do now, so the point in the Biennale was sort of about that.

KAA: What about the future?

FW: I'm becoming much more poetic in these site-specific projects with museum collections, rather than making a strict critique of their collection. My own trajectory and my own thoughts get placed in there, because now I have so much freedom with museums, they just let me do whatever I want. So it becomes much more poetic rather than strictly

fig. 16:
Safe House II
from *Fred Wilson: Speak of Me as I Am*, 2003,
United States Pavilion, 50th Venice Biennale, organized by the List
Visual Arts Center, Massachusetts Institute of Technology, Cambridge.

revealing of the museum and so I'm happy with that direction. When I'm traveling, I write ideas down all the time and so I have a wealth of things to do in the studio, in the gallery environment. So I definitely plan to do that. However, I'm still very much interested in museum collections and what I find in different parts of the world and places, so I don't plan to stop. What's great is I now can choose between the collections, because art museums, look like art museums. I really have no desire to look at art museums' collections, solely, unless of course there is something quirky in the basement. There has to be some other vantage point or environment that I can see a different thing in. And, with all those museum projects, something comes out of that which makes me think about my personal practice, so I have no problem with coming up with ideas for art.

When I first started making the black glass works, the drip pieces, I deliberately didn't tell people much about what I was doing. That's why the names of the pieces are *Drip, Drop, Plop* (fig. 17) and *Drop Dripped*. It's not really telling you much, and that was done on purpose, deliberately. It was a way for me to get totally away from the specificity of the museum collection. I thought: just let whatever is in me flow out of me and analyze it later. As it happens, it is now affecting my museum work, which is great.

I kind of find these glass drips and drops operatic in a certain way. They're kind of over the top, if you're thinking "tears." And the glassblower, Dante Marioni, liked making them. Though he himself does not make forms like that, they're something that he feels comfortable blowing, and that made a big difference. Because when you work with an artisan, they can make anything, but if their way of working flows with your forms, you have a real synergy going on there. He and I get long really well because of that; it doesn't look like his work, but he feels very close to the form. And so that

fig. 17:

Drip, Drop, Plop, 2001
twenty-one blown glass elements
Installation dimensions variable,
approximately 96 x 60 x 60"

was really a lucky thing; we still work together, he's really one of the major glassblowers in the United States, young guy, but major… and so that's how that form came about. Because I don't know anything about glass, I worked with somebody who understood it. And if it hadn't worked for him, I might have just dropped it entirely. But it worked very well. Right now I don't have any other ideas for forms particularly in glass, unless there's something all of a sudden I realize I want to reproduce in black glass like a chandelier, but that to me was a very unusual case as well.

KAA: What about the *Mhole?* That's not like anything else (p. 27).

FW: No, well that's true. I mean I guess that has kind of pushed its way, literally pushed its way in another direction! Well there's this kind of narrative where the drips are dropping from the wall onto the floor basically in spots, and then the floor gets masses them, and then they start rising up again. And the *Mhole* is one of these things rising up and going in directions. Where they're going and what happens to them, that's where I'm going … and *Mhole* is sort of going through the wall. What I liked about *Mhole* is it's kind of connected with something Anish Kapour has done. He's worked with perception, beauty and simple form and I imagine consciousness for a long time—things that I am also interested in—and one of the things he does are these holes—in the ground, in the wall—and it's just basically pigment that makes it look like a flat surface, when actually it's just an empty void. So of course I'm fully aware of that, and had I not done it so that you come around the wall and see this thing with the eyes, it would have been very derivative. But for me it's like a conscious joke on that, or a joke about consciousness in a certain way. So I was thinking about Anish Kapour a bit … I mean I love his work, but this was kind of funny, I mean what is on the other side of the void? the other side of the universe? Would you end up facing yourself?

Viscous Risk, 2005
as installed in *Fred Wilson: Black Like Me*,
The Aldrich Contemporary Art Museum, Ridgefield, Connecticut
twenty-one blown glass elements
Installation dimensions variable, approximately 10 x 17 x 7'

Also I like the fact that if you put your face in it, if you look in, you're looking and you don't realize that there are eyes on the other side looking too!

KAA: So what don't you do? You don't paint?

FW: No.

KAA: And you don't make sculpture any more, well the Drips are sort of sculptures, but you don't make sculpture in the way in which you used to.

FW: Right, I don't build sculpture anymore, I don't carve or anything. I don't see myself doing it. I don't see myself physically doing things. I don't need to actually make things with my hands anymore. I get as much pleasure or more out of the manipulation of ideas, and having them come to fruition in other people's hands … through other people's hands; I have no problem with that.

KAA: But you *have* done performance?

FW: Yes, and I still do performance. But my performances are impromptu, and when I have an idea, I do them, and they sort of happen. I did one recently at Skidmore College, where I was invited to speak. They asked me give some opening remarks for a panel. So I did a little performance that they didn't expect. I would speak about it more, but I'd like to develop it further and do it again somewhere. I like the element of surprise, so I won't speak about it right now.

KAA: But it was also in a way part of your continued tradition of reflection on the museum as a space?

FW: That's right, exactly, and it was completely that. The panel was held in the Tang Museum. There are certain conventions in museum events and conferences that are worth looking into, taking apart. I try to do that with all the media available to me. Performance is particu-

larly useful in the museum environment because it is so out of its element, so unexpected.

KAA: Do you think that the sort of work you've done has had an impact on the way in which curators think about their jobs?

FW: I think so. You know I don't like patting myself on the back, but I mean if what museum curators and directors tell me is true, I think it has made a huge impact, especially with successive generations of curators and directors.

KAA: So what ideas have they taken away from your practice?

FW: Museums move glacially, I mean they don't change overnight. And staffs change, and so ideas disappear as the staff changes. But I think they were already aware of different publics, and they knew they had to find a different public. But the idea that what we do reflects our own point of view, I think that was a new idea. And they don't know what to do with the fact that the public does not necessarily understand a show the way they understand it, or they think they understand it. And I don't know that they have been able to internalize it enough to change so radically, but they certainly do think about it. You know, it would be a nice thing to find out what museums have done that they wouldn't have done before. They tell me, "Yes, this has happened," and, certainly, the places I've worked, small things have happened that have changed. Or the curators, when they go to the next place, they do things slightly differently.

Many museums have a hard time finding a black public. It's hard, it's not an easy task, and they often give up. They just say, "That's too hard." And so we have black children come in, and that will cover it. Or we hire a black PR person, or a black educator … but they don't change their exhibitions at all. That becomes an issue, but I think certain museums try in their way, so that maybe the curators now, and the directors now, have a more enlightened view. But you still have the trustees. And if they don't know why you want to do this, how much can you do? So there's lots of work to do; but as I say in their small ways they are different, even though it's really small and it's not changing visitorship at all. They're buying different things, even MoMA is trying to buy some different things, or are aware that they should. The Whitney's had some small and large exhibitions that they wouldn't have had on a regular basis years ago.

But there are so many different things that they could do, just as far as access goes. They don't even know how to access the so-called "Black Community." But they have a hard time switching gears, because they're forever trying to get wealthy people to give money to the museum—I'm talking all museums—and to do that, you have to be about your master-pieces, and your treasures, and speak so that they will want to be a part of that. That will make wealthy individuals feel that it's worthy of their interest, something they can talk about with their friends on a certain level and perhaps have influence beyond the museum. But then museums also want to talk to the average person, and say "this is really for you," and you need a whole other language for that. And so they're used to one language—the one for the wealthy patrons—and not the other, and the challenge is how to do both. I don't know how you do both. I mean it's a tough row to hoe. The Met gets around this because it has all the treasures and the tourist popula-tion's so vast. But they have the stuff, not so many museums can do that. Armor will bring the average person in, whereas, unless you are a tourist destination like MoMA, art of the 1950s or the 1920s or contemporary art is just not going to bring crowds in on regular basis; it's not that kind of a place. So they do have to play to both. For the money, they've got to play to the wealthy; for the numbers, which the foundations and corporations want to see in order to give them money, they have to have a whole other kind of language.

Mhole, 2005
blown glass
18 x 11 x 11"

KAA: What about other spaces? I mean there are of course a few famous black museums and galleries in New York, and then for contemporary art generally, there are smaller places I guess all around the country.

FW: But they all rely on wealthy patrons, because it's just not something the average person's going to fund, and especially if you're doing things that you don't know if a corporation's going to want to put their name to. It's difficult, and so… of course the smaller institutions, I was going to say they are more inclined to be aware of the need to have other Americans come in, other people come in, but that's really not necessarily true.

This situation not only affects who comes to the museum, but who gets hired and also what gets shown there as well. There's a whole generation of black artists that's gone unnoticed, the one before me, because they were doing a kind of abstraction that's totally not in favor now, and of course it was in favor at one time, but black artists were not.

KAA: They're still working?

FW: Yeah, if they're living, they're still working.

KAA: But you really lived through the transition?

FW: Yeah I'm kind of the link between these young kids who have no clue as to how the art world was when, if you were in the museum as a black person, or at a gallery opening, they thought you were there to collect the cups! Now they have no idea, and… so I'm kind of that link from that past period. Which I, because of my experience as a child, I'm very conscious of. In fact, in my young childhood—where I was the only black child in the neighborhood, and totally misunderstood, and all the racist tropes were going on in popular culture—I really was kind of an outsider within my own community; it was rarely something overt, at school, camp, everything, but it was just there. I see the museum world very much like that, not racist, but so mono-cultural that it is unaware of itself, and so I think that's why I'm so attuned to it.

KAA: Does the new generation, the one that comes after you, draw on your work?

FW: They come to me and it's—talk about being old—they're like, "I studied you in high school. And you're younger than I thought." Okay, good! But, yeah, I mean I think I have affected a lot of them, which I think is great because I know I was affected by artists of that generation slightly older than me. It was rewarding just to see them working as professional artists. That's why I lecture all over the place. Role models are important. I've never particularly felt like one—though I know I am. I think they connect with the fact that I make art about the world as I see it and about my own personal experience. I find myself drawn to difficult issues, you know, the historic, the current and the personal, that I don't see being discussed anywhere. If my work can inspire young artists and offer them new ways of seeing things, then I think that's great. But I know, if nothing else, I have given some young people an ability to imagine a life as an artist.

K. Anthony Appiah, the Laurance S. Rockefeller University Professor of Philosophy and the University Center for Human Values at Princeton, was born in London, England, and raised in Kumasi, Ghana. He studied medical sciences and philosophy at Cambridge University, where he then went on to complete a doctorate in philosophy. He has written widely in the philosophy of mind and language and in African and African-American intellectual history and literary studies, and has focused more recently on ethics and political philosophy. His writing about art has included essays for the Africa show at the Royal Academy and the Guggenheim, pieces for catalogues at the Museum for African Art and the Dia Foundation, and a recent essay on cultural patrimony in the *New York Review of Books*. He books include monographs in the philosophy of mind and language, two introductions to philosophy, three novels, and several books in the philosophy of culture and in ethics and political philosophy; and he is the editor, with Henry Louis Gates Jr., of *Africana: The Encyclopedia of the African and African-American Experience*. His most recent book, *Cosmopolitanism: Ethics in a World of Strangers* argues for the central place of the arts in cross-cultural conversation.

Black Memory, 2005
wood and glass vitrine, fifteen small oil cans, two large oil cans, seventeen ink bottles, one glass bottle
48 x 72 x 46"

FRED WILSON

BORN

1954, Bronx, New York

EDUCATION

1976, State University of New York, Purchase, B.F.A.

SELECTED ONE-ARTIST EXHIBITIONS

1988

Portrait of Audubon, The Public Art Fund, outdoor sculpture, Chambers Street and West Broadway, New York.

1990

The Other Museum, White Columns, New York, May 18–June 10.

1991

The Other Museum, Washington Project for the Arts, Washington D.C., February 9–March 17.

Fred Wilson: Recent Acquisitions, Gracie Mansion Gallery, New York, February 14–March 9.

Primitivism: High and Low, Metro Pictures, New York, March 9–April 6.

1992

Panta Rhei: A Gallery of Ancient Classical Art, Metro Pictures, New York, September 16–October 3.

1992–1993

Mining the Museum: An Installation by Fred Wilson, The Contemporary and Maryland Historical Society, Baltimore, April 4–February 28.

1993

The Spiral of Art History, Indianapolis Museum of Art, Indiana, January 16–March 28.

The Museum: Mixed Metaphors, Seattle Art Museum, Washington, January 28–June 13.

Transformations 4: Fred Wilson, Beaver College Art Gallery, Glenside, Pennsylvania, March 30–April 20.

An Invisible Life: A View into the World of a 120-Year-Old Man, Capp Street Project, San Francisco, August 20–October 3.

1994

OpEd: Fred Wilson, Museum of Contemporary Art, Chicago, April 30–August 21.

'Insight: In Site: In Sight: Incite: Memory,' Artist and the Community: Fred Wilson, South Eastern Center for Contemporary Art, Winston-Salem, North Carolina, August 6–September 28.

1995–1996

Collectibles, Metro Pictures, New York, December 2–January 6.

1996

An Invisible Life: A View into the World of a 120-Year-Old Man, Points of Entry: Three Rivers Arts Festival, Pittsburgh, June 7–23.

1997

Collectibles, Rena Bransten Gallery, San Francisco, March 27–April 26.

Reshuffling the Deck: Selections from the U.C. Davis Collections, Richard L. Nelson Gallery and Fine Arts Collections, University of California, Davis, April 13–May 16.

1998

Viewing the Invisible: An Installation by Fred Wilson, Ian Potter Museum of Art, The University of Melbourne, Australia, October 7–December 6.

1999

Speaking in Tongues: A Look at the Language of Display, M. H. de Young Memorial Museum, Fine Arts Museums of San Francisco, California, January 16–May 2.

Fred Wilson: The Greeting Gallery, organized by Yerba Buena Center for the Arts, M. H. de Young Memorial Museum, Fine Arts Museums of San Francisco, California, January 16–May 2.

2000

Fred Wilson: Drawings and Maquettes for A Light Rail Station, Jersey City Museum, Newark, January 12–March 18.

2001–2004

Fred Wilson, Objects and Installations 1979–2000, Center for Art and Visual Culture, University of Maryland, Baltimore, October 11, 2001–January 12, 2002. Traveled to: Tang Teaching Museum and Art Gallery, Skidmore College, Saratoga Springs, New York, October 26, 2002–January 7, 2003; Berkeley Art

Dark Dawn, 2005 (detail)
as installed in *Fred Wilson: Black Like Me*,
The Aldrich Contemporary Art Museum, Ridgefield, Connecticut
eighteen blown glass elements, five plate glass elements
Installation dimensions variable, approximately 10 x 20 x 7'

Museum and Pacific Film Archive, University of California, January 22–March 3, 2003; Blaffer Gallery, The Art Museum, University of Houston, Texas, May 3–August 3, 2003; Addison Gallery of American Art, Phillips Academy, Andover, Massachusetts, September 3–November 8, 2003; Santa Monica Museum, California, December 5, 2003–February 8, 2004; Studio Museum in Harlem, New York, April 28–July 4, 2004; Chicago Cultural Center, July 24–September 19, 2004.

2002

Is This Now Just Beginning?, Fosdick-Nelson Gallery, Alfred University, Alfred, New York, January 30–February 22.

2003

Fred Wilson: Aftermath, Berkeley Art Museum and Pacific Film Archive, University of California, January 22–November 23.

Fred Wilson: Speak of Me as I Am, United States Pavilion, 50th Venice Biennale, Italy, June 15–November 2.

2005

Fred Wilson: So Much Trouble in the World—Believe It or Not!, Hood Museum of Art, Dartmouth, Hannover, New Hampshire, October 4–December 11.

2005–2006

Fred Wilson: Black Like Me, The Aldrich Contemporary Art Museum, Ridgefield, Connecticut July 10–January 8.

SELECTED GROUP EXHIBITIONS

1981

Festive Works, A.I.R. Gallery, New York.

1982

Ornament as Sculpture, Sculpture Center, New York.

Terminal New York, A.A.A. Art, New York.

Looks at Books, ABC NO Rio, New York.

Grand Army Plaza: Three Sculptors, organized by the Department of Parks, Grand Army Plaza Arch, Brooklyn, New York.

Spare Parts, Materials for the Arts, Department of Cultural Affairs, New York.

1983

The Monument Redefined, Gowanus Memorial Artyard, New York.

After Dark, William Patterson College, Patterson, New Jersey.

1984

Exchange of Sources: Expanding Powers, Real Art Ways, Hartford, Connecticut.

Racist America, Dramatis Personae Gallery, New York.

Sticks and Stones-Modern/Post Modern Sculpture, Kenkeleba Gallery, New York.

L'Esprit Enclyclopedique, Caidoz Gallery, New York.

Art Against Apartheid, window installation, 10 on 8, New York.

1985

Art on the Beach, organized by Creative Time, Battery Park City Landfill, New York.

Forecast: Images of the Future, Kenkeleba Gallery, New York.

Visions, Rediscovered, Castillo Gallery, New York.

1986

The Bronx Celebrates: Alternative Spaces, Lehman College Art Gallery, Bronx, New York.

Ando/Wilson, New Sculpture, John Jay College Art Gallery, New York.

1987

Selections from the Artists File, Artists Space, New York.

Intellects and Idiosyncrasies, 55 Mercer Gallery, New York.

1988

Rooms With a View: The Struggle Betweeen Culture, Content and the Context of Art, Longwood Art Gallery, Bronx Council on the Arts, New York.

1990

Public Mirror: Artists Against Racial Prejudice, Clocktower Gallery, P.S.1 Contemporary Art Center, New York.

The New School Collects: Recent Acquisitions, Parsons School of Design, New York.

Fine Arts Faculty Group Show, Galleries at Fashion Institute of Technology, New York.

Orders, Pyramid Art Center, Rochester, New York.

Notes on the Margin: A Framework in Focus, Gracie Mansion Gallery, New York.

Dream Machinations in America, Minor Injury Gallery, Brooklyn, New York.

Conflict and Resolution, Brownsville Art Gallery Manhattanville College, Purchase, New York.

1991

SITEseeing: Travel and Tourism in Contemporary Art, Whitney Museum of American Art, Federal Reserve Plaza, New York, April 2–June 2.

The Subversive Stitch, Simon Watson Gallery, New York, closed July 27.

Group Show, Metro Pictures, New York, June 29–July 31.

Office Installations, Hillwood Art Museum, Brookville, New York.

Outdoor Sculpture Commission, Department of Parks, Prospect Park, New York.

1992

The Big Nothing Or Le Presque Rien, New Museum of Contemporary Art, New York January 15–April 19; French Cultural Services, New York, January 16–February 28.

Environmental Terror, Fine Arts Gallery, University of Maryland Baltimore County, Catonsville, January 30–March 14. Traveled to: Frostburg State University, Maryland; East Main Street Gallery, Richmond, Virginia.

Inheritance, Los Angeles Contemporary Exhibitions, Los Angeles, May 22–June 21.

Group show, Metro Pictures, New York, June 20–July 31.

Putt-Modernism, Artists Space, New York, August 1–September 27.

Past Imperfect: A Museum Looks At Itself, Parrish Art Museum, Southhampton, New York, August 8–November 11.

Transgressions in the White Cube: Territorial Mappings, USDAN Gallery, Bennington College, Bennington, Vermont, November 17–December 21.

The Order of Things: Toward A Politic of Still Life, organized by Real Art Ways, Widener Gallery, Trinity College, Hartford, Connecticut, Winter.

Rosamund Felsen Clinic, Rosamund Felsen Gallery, Los Angeles.

Translation, Centrum Sztuki Współczesnej Zamek Ujazdowski/Center for Contemporary Art, Warsaw, Poland.

The Jewish Museum's Masked Ball: In Celebration of Purim, The Waldorf-Astoria, New York.

1992–1993

Re:claiming Egypt, 4th International Cairo Bienniale, Egypt, December 19–March 19.

1993

1993 Biennial Exhibition, Whitney Museum of American Art, New York, February 24–June 20.

Projects 40: Readymade Identities, The Museum of Modern Art, New York, April 3–May 18.

Artists Respond: The "New World" Question, Studio Museum in Harlem, New York, May 5–August 22.

Construction in Process 4: My Home is Your Home, The Artists' Museum, Lodz, Poland.

The Rag Trade, The InterArt Center, New York.

1993–1994

The Theater of Refusal: Black Art and Mainstream Criticism, Fine Arts Gallery of the University of California, Irvine, April 8–May 12. Traveled to: Richard L. Nelson Gallery, University of California, Davis, November 7–December 17; University Art Gallery, University of California, Riverside, January 9–February 27.

Ciphers of Identity, Fine Arts Gallery, University of Maryland, Baltimore County, November 12–January 21.

1994

Don't Look Now, Thread Waxing Space, New York, January 22–February 26.

Exhibited, Center for Curatorial Studies, Bard College, Annandale-on-Hudson, New York, April 23–September 2.

Western Artists/African Art, Museum for African Art, New York, May 6–August 7. Traveled to: Knoxville Museum of Art, Tennessee; Crocker Art Museum, Sacramento, California.

Die Orte der Kunst: Der Kunstbetrieb als Kunstwerk, Sprengel Museum, Hannover, Germany, May 29–September 11.

Notational Photographs, Metro Pictures, New York, September 17–October 15.

Crash: Nostalgia for the Absence of Cyberspace, Thread Waxing Space, New York.

1994–1995

Black Male: Representations of Masculinity in Contemporary American Art, Whitney Museum of American Art, New York, November 10–March 5.

Cocido y Crudo, Museo Nacional Centro de Arte Reina Sofia, Madrid, Spain, December 14–March 6.

1994–1996

Transformers: The Art of Multiphrenia, organized by Independent Curators Incorporated, New York. Traveled to: Center for Curatorial Studies, Bard College, Annandale-on-Hudson, New York, September 21–November 13, 1994; Decker Galleries, Maryland Institute College of Art, Baltimore, Maryland, November 17–December 17, 1995; Herbert F. Johnson Museum of Art, Cornell University, Ithaca, New York, January 27–March 26, 1996; Art Gallery of Windsor, Ontario, Canada, June 21–September 9, 1996; Illingworth Kerr Art Gallery, Alberta College of Art and Design, Calgary, Alberta, November 4–November 28, 1996.

1995

Heroes and Heroines: From Myth to Reality, New Jersey Center for Visual Arts, Summit, January 13–February 26.

Configura 2-Dialog der Kulturen-Erfurt 1995, Erfurt, Federal Republic of Germany, June 10–September 10.

1996

Cultural Economies: Histories from the Alternative Arts Movement, Drawing Center, New York, February 24–April 6.

Project Row Houses, Houston, Spring.

Inklusion: Exklusion, Steirischer Herbst 96, Graz, Austria.

Putt-Modernism, The Hyde Collection, Glen Falls, New York.

Fragments: Proposta per a una colleccio de fotografia contemporania, Museu d'Art Contemporani, Barcelona.

Three Rivers Arts Festival, Pittsburgh.

Designation, Galerie & Edition Artelier, Graz, Austria.

1996–1997

Burning Issues: Contemporary African-American Art, Museum of Art, Fort Lauderdale, October 21–January 5.

New Histories, Institute of Contemporary Art, Boston, Massachusetts, October 23, 1996–January 5.

Millennium Eve Dress, Fabric Workshop, Philadelphia, December 6–February 22.

1997

Collected, Photographer's Gallery and British Museum, London, April 26–June 21.

Scene of the Crime, Armand Hammer Museum of Art and Cultural Center, Los Angeles, July 23–October 5.

Museum Studies: Eleven Photographer's Views, High Museum of Art, Atlanta.

Millennium Eve Dress, Contemporary Arts Center, Cincinnati.

1997–1998

Heart, Mind, Body, Soul: American Art in the 1990's, Whitney Museum of American Art, New York, November 26–January 4.

1998

Parasite, Drawing Center, New York, February 21–April 4.

Re-Presentation, Freedom Gallery, Albright College Center for the Arts, Reading, Pennsylvania, October 2–November 20.

Postcards From Black America, Hedendaagse Afrikaans-Amerikaanse Kunst, Boschstraat, the Netherlands.

1999

Through The Looking-Glass: Play Things, Newhouse Center for Contemporary Art, Snug Harbor Cultural Center, Staten Island, New York, April 25–October 3.

Trace, Liverpool Biennial of Contemporary Art, Liverpool, September 24–November 7.

Uniform, Center for Curatorial Studies, Bard College, Annandale-on-Hudson, New York.

Kunstwelten im Dialog von Gauguin zur globalen Gegenwart im Museum Ludwig Köln, Museum Ludwig Köln, Cologne.

1999–2000

To the Rescue: Eight Artists in an Archive, organized by Lookout for the American Jewish Joint Distribution Committee, New York. Traveled to: International

Center of Photography, New York, February 12–
May 16; Miami Art Museum, Florida, September 15–
November 28; Contemporary Arts Museum,
Houston, October 7–December 3.

The Museum as Muse: Artists Reflect, The Museum
of Modern Art, New York, March 14–June 1.
Traveled to: Museum of Contemporary Art, San
Diego, September 26–January 9.

2000

Group Show, Metro Pictures, January 18–April 15.

Outbound: Passages From the 90's, Contemporary
Arts Museum, Houston, March 3–May 7.

2000–2001

Juvenilia, Yerba Buena Center for the Arts, San
Francisco, November 4–January 28.

2001

*Play's The Thing: Critical and Transgressive Practices
in Contemporary Art*, organized by the Whitney
Museum of American Art Independent Study
Program, Art Gallery of The Graduate Center, City
University of New York, May 25–July 8.

W, Musée des Beaux-Arts, Dole, France,
June 22–September 30.

*Crossing the Line: Site Specific Works by Fifty Artists
throughout Queens*, Queens Museum of Art, New
York, June 24–October 7.

Museum as Subjects, National Museum of Art,
Osaka, Japan, October 25–December 11.

2001–2002

Group Show, Metro Pictures, New York,
December 8–January 12.

2001–2003

*Pictures, Patents, Monkeys, and More...On
Collecting*, organized by Independent Curators
International, New York. Traveled to: Western
Gallery, Western Washington University,
Bellingham, January 19– March 10, 2001; John
Michael Kohler Arts Center, Sheboygan,
Wisconsin, August 12–October 21, 2001; Akron Art
Museum, Ohio, November 17, 2001– February 18,
2002; Fuller Museum of Art, Brockton,
Massachusetts, June 1–August 18, 2002; Institute
of Contemporary Art, University of Pennsylvania,

Philadelphia, September 4–December 15, 2002;
Pittsburgh Center for the Arts, Pennsylvania,
June 1– August 6, 2003.

2002–2003

Art Inside Out, Children's Museum of Manhattan,
October 10, 2002–December 31, 2003 (extended to
June 4, 2004).

2003

*.mov: Works from the Eyebeam Moving Image
Studios '03*, Eyebeam, New York, January 6–24.

Drawings, Metro Pictures, New York, March 29–
April 26.

*Black President: The Art and Legacy of Fela
Anikulapo-Kuti*, New Museum of Contemporary
Art, New York, July 11–September 28.

2003–2004

*Only Skin Deep: Changing Visions of the American
Self*, International Center of Photography, New
York, December 12–February 29.

2004

Art by MacArthur Fellows, Carl Solway Gallery,
Cincinnati, Ohio, May 7–July 31.

2004–2005

*Common Ground: Discovering Community in 150
Years of Art, Selections from the Collection of Julia
J. Norrell*, Corcoran Gallery of Art, Washington, D.C.,
October 23–January 31.

2005

*Double Consciousness: Black Conceptual Art Since
1970*, Contemporary Arts Museum, Houston,
January 21–April 17.

20 x 20 Art Sale, exhibition and benefit auction for
Bill T. Jones/Arnie Zane Dance Company, organized
by Bill T. Jones and Diane von Furstenberg, Diane
von Furstenberg the Theater, New York, May 10–14.

Very Early Pictures, Luckman Gallery, California
State University, Los Angeles, May 26–July 23.
Traveled to: Arcadia University Art Gallery,
Glenside, Pennsylvania, August 26–October 30.

Summer Group Show, PaceWildenstein, 534 West
25th Street, New York, July 14–August 25.

SELECTED COLLABORATIONS

1976

Dancer/Choreographer; *Sculpturedance*, Roy T. Neuberger Museum, Purchase, New York.

1982

Sculptor (with Julia Demaree, performance artist, and Helene Brandt, sculptor), *A Performance Response to Machines and Sanctuaries*, Sculpture Center, New York.

1983

Tap dancer (with Jane Goldberg), *Dance Environments*, P.S.1 Contemporary Art Center, New York.

1984

Playwright (with Daryl Chan), *Art and The Actor*, Theatre for The New City, New York.

1985

Art on The Beach (with Yoshiko Chuma and Lenny Pickett), Creative Time, Battery Park City Landfill New York.

1987

AvantGardeArama, P.S.122, New York.

1992

Houses of Spirit/Memories of Ancestors: An Outdoor Sculpture Exhibition, Woodlawn Cemetery, New York.

SELECTED AWARDS

1987

New York Foundation for the Arts Fellowship in Sculpture.

1990

New York State Council on the Arts.
National Endowment for the Arts.

1991

New York Foundation for the Arts Fellowship in Sculpture.

1999

The MacArthur Foundation Genius Grant, Chicago.

2002

10th Larry Aldrich Foundation Award, The Aldrich Museum of Contemporary Art, Ridgefield, Connecticut.

2003

American Representative at the United States Pavilion, 50th Venice Biennale, Italy.

Distinguished Visiting Fellow in Object, Exhibition, and Knowledge, Skidmore College, Saratoga Springs, New York.

SELECTED BIBLIOGRAPHY
CATALOGUES AND BROCHURES

1987

Selections from the Artists File (exhibition catalogue). Essay by Kellie Jones. New York: Artists Space, 1987.

1991

The Other Museum (exhibition brochure). Washington, D.C.: Washington Project for the Arts, 1991.

1992

Past Imperfect: A Museum Looks At Itself (exhibition catalogue). Essays by Maurice Berger, Alan Wallach and Judith Barry. Southhampton, New York: Parrish Art Museum, 1992.

Re:claiming Egypt (exhibition brochure). Essay by Kathleen Goncharov. Cairo: International Cairo Bienniale, 1992.

1993

1993 Biennial Exhibition (exhibition catalogue). New York: Whitney Museum of American Art, 1993.

The Museum: Mixed Metaphors (exhibition catalogue). Essay by Patterson Sims. Seattle: Seattle Art Museum, 1993.

The Spiral of Art History (exhibition brochure). Indianapolis: Indianapolis Museum of Art, 1993.

Transformations 4: Fred Wilson (exhibition brochure). Essay by Lois Nesbitt. Glenside, Pennsylvania: Beaver College Art Gallery, 1993.

1994

Corrin, Lisa G., ed. *Mining the Museum: An Installation by Fred Wilson* (exhibition catalogue). New York: The New Press, 1994.

Golden, Thelma. *Black Male: Representations of Masculinity in Contemporary American Art* (exhibition catalogue). New York: Whitney Museum of American Art, 1994.

'*Insight: In Site: In Sight: Incite: Memory,*' *Artist and the Community: Fred Wilson* (exhibition catalogue). Texts by Susan Lubowsky, John C. Larson and Jeff Fleming. Winston-Salem, North Carolina: South Eastern Center for Contemporary Art, 1994.

OpEd: Fred Wilson (exhibition catalogue). Essay by Nadine Wasserman. Chicago: Museum of Contemporary Art, 1994.

1995

Cooke, Lynne and Peter Wollen, ed. *Visual Display: Culture Beyond Appearances*. New York: Dia Center for the Arts, 1995.

Cocido y Crudo (exhibition catalogue). Madrid: Museo Nacional Centro de Arte Reina Sofía, 1995.

1996

Gangitano, Lia and Steven Nelson, ed. *New Histories* (exhibition catalogue). Boston: The Institute of Contemporary Art, 1996.

1997

Insite97: Private Time In Public Space. Essays by Susan Buck-Morss, Néster García Canclini, George E. Lewis and José Manuel Valenzuela Arce. San Diego: Installation Gallery, 1997.

Lippard, Lucy R. *The Lure of the Local Senses of Place in a Multicentered Society*. New York: New Press, 1997.

Rugoff, Robert. *Scene of the Crime* (exhibition catalogue). Cambridge, Massachusetts: MIT Press, 1997.

1998

Viewing the Invisible: An Installation by Fred Wilson (exhibition catalogue). Essay by Rachel Kent. Conversation with Dr. Gaye Sculthorpe and Tom Mosby. Melbourne, Australia: Ian Potter Museum of Art, 1998.

1999

Dubin, Steven C. *Displays of Power: Controversy in the American Museum from the Enola Gay to Sensation*. New York: New York University Press, 1999.

Fred Wilson: The Greeting Gallery (exhibition catalogue). Essay by Arnold J. Kem. San Francisco: Yerba Buena Center for the Arts, 1999.

Lippard, Lucy R. *On the Beaten Track: Tourism, Art, and Place*. New York: New Press, 1999.

McShine, Kynaston. *The Museum as Muse: Artists Reflect* (exhibition catalogue). New York: The Museum of Modern Art, 1999.

Preble, Duane. *Artforms*. New York: Longman, 1999.

Speaking in Tongues: A Look at the Language of Display (exhibition brochure). San Francisco: M. H. de Young Memorial Museum, 1999.

They Thought It Was She (exhibition catalogue). Texts by Emma Thomas and Anthony Tibbles. Interview by Alex Coles. London: Liverpool Biennial, 1999.

To the Rescue: Eight Artists in an Archive (exhibition catalogue). New York: Lookout for the American Jewish Joint Distribution Committee, 1999.

Wilson, Fred. "About Face II." In *When Pain Strikes*. Minneapolis: Universtiy of Minnesota Press, 1999.

2000

Fred Wilson: Drawings and Maquettes For A Light Rail Station (exhibition brochure). Interview by Alejandro Anreus. Jersey City, New Jersey: Jersey City Museum, 2000.

Hills, Patricia. *Modern Art in the USA: Issues and Controversies of the 20th Century*. Upper Saddle River, New Jersey: Prentice Hall, 2000.

Suderburg, Erika, ed. *Space, Site, Intervention: Situating Installation Art*. Minneapolis: University of Minnesota Press, 2000.

2001

American Visionaries: Selections from the Whitney Museum of American Art. New York: Whitney Museum of American Art, 2001.

Berger, Maurice. *Fred Wilson: Objects and Installations, 1979–2000* (exhibition catalogue). Texts by Jennifer González and Fred Wilson. Baltimore, Maryland: Center for Art and Visual Culture, University of Maryland, Baltimore County; New York: Distributed by D.A.P.; Distributed Art Publishers, 2001.

Hassan, Salah and Iftikhar Dadi, ed. *Unpacking Europe*. Rotterdam: Museum Boijmans Van Beuningen, 2001.

Hatch, James V., ed. *Artist and Influence*. New York: Hatch-Billops Collection, 2001.

Heartney, Eleanor. *Postmodernism*. London: Tate Publishing, 2001.

Ivey, Bill. *A Creative Legacy: A History of the National Endowment fo the Arts Visual Artists' Fellowship Program*. New York: Harry N. Abrams, 2001.

Museum as Subjects. Osaka, Japan: The National Museum of Art, 2001.

Newman, Amy. *On the Needs of Visual Artists: A Roundtable 2001*. Colorado Springs, Colorado: The Marie Walsh Sharpe Art Foundation, 2001.

Pictures, Patents, Monkeys, and More...On Collecting (exhibition catalogue). Essays by Ingrid Schaffner, Fred Wilson, and Werner Muensterberger. New York: Independent Curators International, 2001.

Play's The Thing: Critical and Transgressive Practices in Contemporary Art (exhibition catalogue). New York: Whitney Museum of American Art, 2001.

Preble, Duane and Sarah Preble. *Artforms*. Upper Saddle River, New Jersey: Prentice Hall, 2001.

Putnam, James. *Art and Artifact: The Museum as Medium*. London: Thames & Hudson, 2001.

Sturken, Marita and Lisa Cartwright. *Practices of Looking*. New York: Oxford University Press, 2001.

2002

Chuhan, Jagjit et al. *Re:Trace Dialogues*, Liverpool: Liverpool School of Art and Design, 2002.

Doss, Erika. *Twentieth-Century American Art*. Oxford, United Kingdom: Oxford University Press, 2001.

MacClancy, Jeremy, ed. *Exotic No More*. Chicago: University of Chicago Press, 2002.

Osborne, Peter, ed. *Conceptual Art*. London: Phaidon Press, 2002.

Stapp, William F. *Portrait of the Art World: A Century of Art News Photographs*. Washington, D.C.: National Portrait Gallery, Smithsonian Institution, 2002.

2003

Buskirk, Martha. *The Contingent Object of Contemporary Art*. Cambridge, Massachusetts: MIT Press, 2003.

Fred Wilson: Speak of Me as I Am (exhibition catalogue). Essays by Paul H.D. Kaplan and Salah Hassan. Interview by Kathleen Goncharov. Boston: MIT List Visual Arts Center, 2003.

Harris, Michael D. *Colored Pictures: Race and Visual Representation*. Chapel Hill, North Carolina: The University of North Carolina Press, 2003.

2005

Double Consciousness: Black Conceptual Art Since 1970 (exhibition catalogue). Houston: The Contemporary Arts Museum, 2005.

2006

Conversations: Among Friends featuring Fred Wilson and Robert Storr (lecture brochure). Essay by Robert Storr. New York: The Museum of Modern Art, 2006.

SELECTED BIBLIOGRAPHY PERIODICALS

1988

Fisher, Jean. "Rooms With A View: B.C.A. Longwood Art Gallery" (exhibition review). *Artforum* (March 1987): 137.

1990

Karmel, Pepe. "Art in Review: Fred Wilson: Collectibles" (exhibition review). *The New York Times*, 12 January 1990: C31.

Levin, Kim. "Bad Timing" (exhibition review). *The Village Voice*, 6 March 1990: 102.

Levin, Kim. "Turning the Tables" (exhibition review). *The Village Voice*, 19 June 1990: 116.

Nesbitt, Lois E. "Fred Wilson: White Columns" (exhibition review). *Artforum* (October 1990): 172.

1991

Balken, Debra Bricker. "Fred Wilson at Gracie Mansion and Metro Pictures" (exhibition reviews). *Art in America* (July 1991): 113–114.

Berger, Maurice. "On Nationality: 13 Artists." *Art in America* (September 1991): 131–132.

Decter, Joshua. "Fred Wilson at Metro Pictures" (exhibition review). *Arts Magazine* (Summer 1991): 92.

Kimmelman, Michael. "Fred Wilson: Metro Pictures" (exhibition review). *The New York Times*, 22 March 1991: C19.

Mahoney, Robert. "Fred Wilson at Gracie Mansion" (exhibition review). *Arts Magazine* (May 1991): 98–99.

Schildkrout, Enid. "Ambiguous Messages and Ironic Twists: Into the Heart of Africa and The Other Museum." *Museum Anthropology* (Flagstaff, Arizona) 15 (May 1991): 16–23.

1992

Als, Hilton. "The Ghosts in the Museum. Artist Fred Wilson Mines History." *The Village Voice*, 22 September 1992: 41.

Cameron, Dan. "Art and Politics: The Intricate Balance." *Art & Auction* (November 1992): 76, 78, 80.

Cassedy, Susannah. "The Museum Mine Field." *Museum Notes* (July/August 1992): 12–14.

Coles, Robert. "Whose Museums?" *American Art* (Washington, D.C.) Winter 1992: 6–11.

Dorsey, John. "Mining the Stores of History with a New Mind-Set." *The Sun* (Baltimore), 5 April 1992: 1+.

Kelleran, David. "Fred Wilson at Metro Pictures" (exhibition review). *Flash Art* (November/ December 1992): 98.

Kimmelman, Michael. "An Improbable Marriage of Artist And Museum." *The New York Times*, 2 August 1992: 27.

Klein, Julia M. "Mining the Museum Hangs Galleries with Their Own Rope." *Philadephia Inquirer*, 2 June 1992: C3.

Kuspit, Donald. "The Magic Kingdom of the Museum." *Artforum* (April 1992): 58–63.

Lewis, Jo Ann. "Coming Out From the Shadows of History." *Washington Post*, 30 August 1992: G1, G6.

McGovern, Adam. "Fred Wilson: Metro Pictures" (exhibition review). *Cover Magazine* (December 1992).

Tanguy, Sarah "Fred Wilson, Maryland Historical Society" (exhibition review). *Sculpture* (September/October 1992): 76.

Wallach, Amei. "A Vision of Green." *New York Newsday*, 24 March 1992: 54–55.

Wilson, Fred. "Mining the Museum" (portfolio). *Grand Street*, no. 44: 151–172.

1993

Barcott, Bruce. "Mixed-up Museum." *Seattle Weekly*, 10 February 1993: 35–39.

Bonetti, David. "The Secrets of a Magical History Tour." *San Francisco Examiner*, 27 August 1993: E10–E11.

Brumfield, John. "Marginalia: Life in a Day of Black L.A. or, The Theater of Refusal." *Art Issues* 29 (September/October 1993): 24–27.

Corrin, Lisa G. "Mining the Museum: An Installation Confronting History" (exhibition review). *Curator* (December 1993): 302–313.

Garfield, Donald. "Making the Museum Mine: An Interview with Fred Wilson." *Museum News* 72 (May/June 1993): 46+.

Glowen, Ron. "Canon Fodder; Fred Wilson at the Seattle Art Museum" (exhibition review). *Artweek*, 8 April 1993: 29.

Hackett, Regina. "Artist Challenges How Museums Treat Culture" (exhibition review). *Seattle Post-Intelligencer*, 2 February 1993: C1.

Helfand, Glen. "Victorian Secrets." *SF Weekly*, 1 September 1993: 17.

Hoffman, Nan. "Artist Finds IMA's Soul." *Indianapolis News*, 21 January 1993: F15.

"Politically Correct Museums" (exhibition review). *The Economist*, 16–22 January 1993: 85–86.

Mannheimer, Ron. "Positioning is Key to Questioning Museums." *Indianapolis Star*, 24 January 1993.

Mittenthal, Robert. "Fred Wilson: Mixed Metaphors at S.A.M." (exhibition review). *Reflex* (January/ February 1993): 14–15.

Smith, Joan. "Invisible Man Sited." *San Francisco Examiner*, 18 August 1993: C-1, C-4.

Wallach, Amei. "Art with an Attitude." *New York Newsday*, 5 March 1993: 52–53.

1994

Buskirk, Martha. "Interviews with Sherrie Levine, Louise Lawler, and Fred Wilson." *October* 70 (Fall 1994): 109–112.

Corrin, Lisa G. "Installing History." *Art Papers* (May/June 1994): 6–14.

Cotter, Holland. "African Genesis: What Western Artists Like." *The New York Times*, 27 May 1994.

Greenberg, Reesa. "Making Up Museums: Revisionism and Fred Wilson." *Parachute* 76 (October/November/December 1994).

Hess, Elizabeth. "Visible Man." *The Village Voice*, 22 November 1994: 31–34.

Liebermann, Lisa. "[The Acquiring Mind] Africa, at the Source" (exhibition review). *The New York Times Magazine*, 10 July 1994: 46–49.

Paice, Kim. "Book Review-Mining the Museum: An Installation by Fred Wilson." *World Art* 1, no. 2 (1994): 90–91.

Patterson, Tom. "Exhibits Challenge Viewers to Rethink Cultural Assumptions." *Winston-Salem Journal*, 4 September 1994: C3.

Silverthorne, Jeanne. "Mining the Museum: An Installation by Fred Wilson" (book review). *Artforum* (November 1994).

Stamets, Bill. "Conceptual Artist Has His Way With MCA's 'Dreaming' Show." *Chicago Sun Times*, 26 June 1994: B2.

Thorson, Alice. "Fred Wilson Puts Extra Thoughts Into Museum Displays." *Kansas City Star*, 22 May 1994.

Wallach, Amei. "The Shock of the Old." *New York Newsday*, 2 June 1994, Section B.

1995

Halle, Howard. "Interview: Race Matters." *Time Out New York*, 6–13 December 1995.

James, Curtia. "Remembering Old Salem" (exhibition review). *Art Papers* (July/ August 1995): 28–31.

Reid, Calvin. "Caught in Flux." *Transition* (Spring 1995): 134–135.

Wilson, Fred. "Silent Messages." *Museums Journal* (London) (May 1995): 27–29.

1996

Colman, David. "Pretty on the Outside: A New Breed of Black Artists Launches a Fresh Debate on Race with Works That Look Lovely but Bite Back." *George* (June/July 1996): 117–118.

Cromwell, Kathleen. "Fred Wilson: Metro Pictures" (exhibition review). *Flash Art* (May/June 1996): 114.
Demos, T. J. "Fred Wilson: Metro Pictures" (exhibition review). *New Art Examiner*, March 1996: 42–43.

González, Jennifer. "Fred Wilson: Metro Pictures, New York" (exhibition review). *Frieze* (London) (May 1996): 62–63.

Hess, Elizabeth. "Jemimas on My Mind" (exhibition review). *The Village Voice*, 2 January 1996: 66.

Sirmans, M. Franklin. "Fred Wilson: Metro Pictures" (exhibition review). *Art News* (March 1996): 116.

Smith, Roberta. "Art in Review: Fred Wilson" (exhibition review). *The New York Times*, 12 January 1996: C31.

von Ziegesar, Peter. "Fred Wilson at Metro Pictures" (exhibition review). *Art in America* (June 1996): 103–104.

Whitfield, Tony. "Fred Wilson: Mining the Memory." *Sphere* (Spring 1996): 17–18.

1997

Barrett, David. "Collected: Photographer's Gallery, London." *Frieze* (London) (September/October 1997): 96–97.

Gordon, Allan M. "Fred Wilson at UC Davis" (exhibition review). *Artweek* (San Jose) 28 (June 1997): 21–22.

Kent, Rachel. "Fred Wilson: The Fine Art of Subversion." *Art Monthly* (Melbourne) (April 1997): 18–19.

Williams, Gilda. "Irredeemable Skeletons" (exhibition catalogue). *Art Monthly* (London) (May 1997): 32–34.

1998

MacAdam, Barbara A. "Fred Wilson." *Art News* (March 1998): 167.

1999

Kimmelman, Michael. "When Artists Dress Up Modern Jewish History" (exhibition review). *The New York Times*, 26 February 1999: E37, E44.

MacFarquhar, Neil. "32 Receive Grants From MacArthur Foundation." *The New York Times*, 23 June 1999: A15.

Saltz, Jerry. "Inside Job" (exhibition review). *The Village Voice*, 18 May 1999: 141.

Stafford, Amy. "Second Thought: Art @ the Millennium." *Surface*, no. 12: 126–130.

2000

Bless, Nancy. "Welcome Home: Project Row Houses," *Sculpture* 19 (June 2000): 32–39.

Johnson, Patricia C. "'Outbound' Captures Moments of a Decade" (exhibition review). *Houston Chronicle*, 18 March 2000: 7–8.

Klaasmeyer, Kelly. "Caution: Swoon Zone" (exhibition review). *Houston Press* (April 2000): 71–72.

Newkirk, Pamela. "Object Lessons: Fred Wilson Reinstalls Museum Collections to Highlight Sins of Omission." *Art News* (January 2000): 156–159.

Shottenkirk, Dena. "Four on the Floor." *International Contemporary Art* (Summer 2000): 44.

2001

Berwick, Carly. "The Changing of the Guards." *Art News* (March 2001): 148–151.

Dawson, Jessica. "The Dark Side of Museums." *Washington Post*, 8 November 2001.

2002

Graeber, Laurel. "Family Fare: A Journey Into Art." *The New York Times*, 8 November 2002: E42.

Schmerler, Sarah. "Venetian Find" (exhibition review). *Time Out New York*, 7–14 November 2002: 85.

Vogel, Carol. "Heading For Venice 2003." *The New York Times*, 25 October 2002: E32.

Wong, Sherry. "Artnet News-Wilson to Venice Biennale." *www.artnet.com*, November 2002.

2003

Allen, Jane Ingram. "Shifts in Meaning: A Conversation with Fred Wilson." *Sculpture* (May 2003): 40–45.

Baker, Kenneth. "Creating Art Out of Artifacts." *San Francisco Chronicle*, 23 January 2003: E1, E9.

Coleman, David. "A Lost Patrimony Comes Home." *The New York Times*, 25 May 2003: N8.

"Fred Wilson Wins Aldrich Foundation Award." *Sculpture* (January/February 2003): 15.

Helfand, Glen. "Object Lesson." *San Francisco Bay Guardian*, 22 January 2003: 36–37.

Helfand, Glen. "Fred Wilson, Berkeley Art Museum." *Artforum* (May 2003): 174–175.

Knight, Christopher. "Fred Wilson: Reading Between the Lines" (exhibition review). *Los Angeles Times*, 24 December 2003.

Madoff, Steven Henry. "How Do You Get to the Biennale? Apply." *The New York Times*, 1 June 2003: AR35.

Miles, Christopher. "Venice by Way of Africa." *Los Angeles Times*, 20 July 2003: E42.

Pollack, Barbara. "Deft in Venice." *The Village Voice*, 12 June 2003.

Putnam, James. "The Quest for Othello." *Modern Painters* (Summer 2003): 94–97.

Robinson, Dorothy. "Masked Masks and Whipping Posts." *Berkeleyan* (University of California, Berkeley), 30 January 2003: 3.

Schmerler, Sarah. "The Lone Rearranger." *Art Review*, June 2003: 60–63.

Vetrocq, Marcia E. "Venice Biennale: 'Every Idea But One.'" *Art in America* (September 2003): 76–84.

2004

Brown, Kathan. "Overview: Fred Wilson." *Crown Point Press Newsletter* (May 2004).

Cotter, Holland. "Pumping Air Into the Museum, So It's as Big as the World Outside" (exhibition review). *The New York Times*, 30 April 2004: E31.

Goodbody, Bridget L. "Black Like Who?" *Time Out New York*, 20–27 May 2004: 66.

Hassan, Salah M. "Fred Wilson's Black Venezia: Fictitious Histories And Notion Of Truth." *NKA Journal of Contemporary African Art*, (Summer 2004): 12–19.

Hudson, Suzanne. "Fred Wilson, Studio Museum in Harlem" (exhibition review). *Artforum* (November 2004): 223.

2005

Streitfeld, L. P. "Fred Wilson's Evoltionary Leap into a Perfect Marriage" (exhibition review). *The Advocate & Greenwich Time*, 4 September 2005: D3, D4.

Wilson, Fred. "Fred Wilson In the Hood," interview with Barbara Thompson. *Hood Museum of Art Quarterly, Dartmouth College*, autumn 2005: 4–5.

SELECTED PUBLIC COLLECTIONS

Baltimore Museum of Art, Maryland

Birmingham Museum of Art, Alabama

Denver Art Museum, Colorado

Jewish Museum, New York

Kresge Art Museum, Michigan State University, East Lansing

Memphis Brooks Museum of Art, Tennessee

Montclair Art Museum, New Jersey

The Museum of Modern Art, New York

New School University, New York

Seattle Art Museum, Washington

Whitney Museum of American Art, New York

Page 2:
Chandelier Mori: Speak of Me as I Am, 2003 (detail)
Murano glass and light bulbs
70 x 67 x 67"

Photography:
Courtesy the artist; p. 8 (fig. 4)
Courtesy the artist and Bronx Council on the Arts; p. 8 (figs. 3, 5)
Jeff Goldman, The Contemporary and Maryland
Historical Society, Baltimore; p. 5
Aram Jibilan; p. 19
Ellen Labenski; pp. 2, 9 (fig. 8), 20–21, 24, 25, 27, 29, 31
Kerry Ryan McFate; pp. 6, 9 (figs. 6, 7)
Jeffrey Nintzel; p. 22
R. Ransick/A. Cocchi; pp. 13, 17, 20 (fig. 13), 23

Design:
Tomo Makiura

Production:
Paul Pollard
Tucker Capparell
Motohiko Tokuta

Printing:
Meridian Printing, East Greenwich, Rhode Island

ISBN: 1-930743-59-9